THE PERFECT
AFTERNOON TEA
BOOK

THE PERFECT
Afternoon Tea
BOOK

LORENZ BOOKS
LONDON • SYDNEY • NEW YORK • BATH

This edition first published in 1997 by Lorenz Books

© Anness Publishing Limited 1997

Lorenz Books is an imprint of Anness Publishing Limited
Hermes House, 88–89 Blackfriars Road,
London SE1 8HA

This edition distributed in Canada by
Raincoast Books
8680 Cambie Street, Vancouver,
British Columbia V6P 6M9

ISBN 1 85967 542 5

Publisher Joanna Lorenz
Senior Cookery Editor Linda Fraser
Series Editor Sarah Ainley
Designers Patrick McLeavey & Hannah Attwell
Illustrator Anna Koska
Photographers Michelle Garrett, Amanda Heywood &
Debbie Patterson
Recipes Carole Clements, Tessa Evelegh,
Carole Handslip, Gilly Love, Liz Trigg &
Elizabeth Wolf-Cohen

For all recipes, quantities are given in both metric and
imperial measures, and, where appropriate, measures are
also given in standard cups and spoons. Follow one set, but
not a mixture, because they are not interchangeable.

Printed and bound in China
1 3 5 7 9 10 8 6 4 2

Contents

Introduction

Most us us don't often have time to pause in our busy lives and enjoy taking tea, so on the special days when we do this charming meal can be a particular treat. The very words "afternoon tea" are evocative of holidays and weekends: tea on the lawn during a long leisurely summer's day in the garden, or by the fire after a frosty winter walk, when there is nothing more welcoming than the aroma of freshly baked scones or hot buttered toast. Teatime is a relaxing, sociable event that everyone looks forward to hungrily, and it's especially satisfying to cosset your family and friends by providing home-made treats to make it a memorable occasion.

Afternoon tea is a flexible meal: a plate of tiny sandwiches or pretty biscuits to accompany a pot of delicately flavoured China tea may be all that is needed, but if you've worked up a hearty appetite after a day's gardening, some strenuous sport or a long walk, tea might feature more substantial fare. Boiled or scrambled eggs, perhaps, savoury pâtés or slices of home-baked ham with piquant chutneys, are traditional elements of an old-fashioned "high tea". With lots of fresh crusty bread and jam, a rich chocolate cake or a fruit tart, this kind of tea does more than fill the hungry gap between lunch and supper — it's quite capable of replacing one or other of those meals altogether.

Ever since the drinking of tea began, it has been surrounded by ceremony and formality, and this tradition is just as enjoyable today. Set the scene for an elegant tea with a sparkling tablecloth and proper napkins, and use your best and prettiest cups and saucers. It really is true that tea tastes better when it's drunk from a fine china cup. Try to use proper leaf tea rather than tea-bags, and brew it with care so that it is truly delicious and refreshing. If you are making sandwiches, make sure the fillings look as irresistible as they will taste, remove the crusts and cut them small so that everyone has room for more.

Fresh, still-warm scones and muffins are perfect vehicles for your own home-made jams and jellies, delicious with lashings of clotted cream. For summer teas in the garden, infuse the food with the scent of flowers: rose petals and lavender will add magic to preserves, biscuits

and cakes, and taste wonderful accompanied by a subtly perfumed tea such as Earl Grey or Rose Poochong. For a really original, and highly romantic, effect, try heart-shaped rose-petal sandwiches.

If you are planning a grand tea party this book will provide all the suggestions you need to make your table groan with mouth-watering delights. But even if you don't relish the idea of baking on such a scale, any one of the delicious ideas in this book would make a simple teatime special. All of the recipes are clearly presented and easy to follow.

Everyone loves the welcoming smell of baking. Satisfied smiles around the tea-table are guaranteed and will amply reward your efforts.

7

Teas

ASSAM

Strong, full-bodied Indian tea with a powerful malty flavour and a rich golden colour. Assam is recommended for cold winter days and first thing in the morning, and is a major ingredient of the various blends known as "English Breakfast Tea". Serve with milk.

CEYLON

Of the various teas from Sri Lanka, the "high-grown" types are the best quality. Golden in colour and of medium strength, Ceylon tea is excellent with or without milk, and is also very good iced, for a refreshing drink on a hot summer's afternoon.

DARJEELING

Sometimes called the "Champagne of Teas", the best Darjeeling is grown high in the foothills of the Himalayas, and makes a light, fragrant tea with a subtle Muscat aroma. Drink it with milk or lemon. It makes a very good iced tea.

EARL GREY

A blend of black China teas created for the second Earl Grey in the 1830s, scented with oil of bergamot. Earl Grey is pale and refreshing with or without milk, or with a slice of lemon.

FORMOSA OOLONG

A pale golden, aromatic tea, formosa oolong is best drunk without milk, sugar or lemon to appreciate its distinctive flavour.

GUNPOWDER GREEN

The best-known green China tea, so-called because its dry rolled leaves were thought to resemble gunpowder. The leaves of Gunpowder Green unfurl when infused. The fragrant, pale tea, best drunk without milk, is particularly low in caffeine.

8

JASMINE

The dried flowers of the scented white jasmine are added to black or green tea to make a fragrant drink that is traditionally served as a digestive after a meal.

LAPSANG SOUCHONG

The large leaves of this black China tea acquire their distinctive flavour by being smoked in baskets over oak chips. Best served with only a little or no milk.

ROSE POUCHONG

A black China tea scented with natural rose oil. A lovely summer drink.

BREWING THE PERFECT CUP OF TEA

1 Use fresh, good quality tea, which should always be kept in an airtight container.

2 Fill the kettle with freshly drawn cold water and bring it to the boil. Meanwhile, warm the teapot, preferably china or earthenware, by rinsing it with hot water, so that the boiling water is not cooled as it touches the tea leaves.

3 Put in 1 teaspoon of tea leaves per person, adding an extra spoonful "for the pot" if you like your tea strong.

4 Take the teapot to the kettle and pour the water over the tea as soon as it comes to the boil. Stir briefly, put on the lid, and leave to brew for 3–5 minutes. Stir again before pouring the tea.

Techniques

USING YEAST

There are three main types of yeast available — easy-blend, dried and fresh. Add easy-blend yeast to the dry ingredients directly from the packet; there is no need to dissolve it in liquid first. Bread made with this kind of yeast can be shaped after mixing and given only one rising. Dried yeast should be sprinkled into the warm liquid together with a pinch of sugar. Stir well and set aside in a warm place for about 10–15 minutes. If the liquid in your recipe is milk, it will need about 30 minutes. When the yeast liquid becomes frothy, stir into the dry ingredients. Place fresh yeast in a small bowl with a pinch of sugar and a little lukewarm water. Cream together until smooth, then leave for 5–10 minutes until frothy before adding to the dry ingredients.

LINING BAKING TINS

To line a round tin, place the tin on grease-proof or non-stick baking paper and draw round it. Cut out two circles, then cut a strip of paper a little longer than the tin's circumference and one and a half times its depth. Grease the tin and place one paper circle in the base. Make diagonal cuts along the paper edge. Line the side of the tin with the strip, with the snipped fringe overlapping the base. Place the second paper circle in the base of the tin, covering the fringe. Lightly grease the paper.

To line a loaf tin, cut a strip of baking paper three times as long as the depth of the tin and as wide as the length of the base. Lightly grease the tin. Place the strip of paper in the tin so that it covers the base and comes up over both long sides.

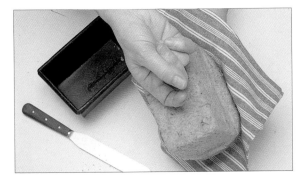

TESTING CAKES AND BREAD

To test if a fruit cake is ready, push a skewer into it: the cake is cooked if the skewer comes out clean. Leave the cake to cool in the tin for 30 minutes. Then turn it out carefully, peel away the lining paper and place on a wire rack.

To test if a sponge cake is ready, press down lightly in the centre of the cake with your fingertips – if the cake springs back it is done. Loosen around the edge of the tin with a palette knife. Invert the cake on to a wire rack, cover with a second rack, then invert again. Remove the top rack and leave to cool.

To test if a loaf of bread is ready, loosen the edges of the loaf with a palette knife, then tip the bread out of the tin. Hold the loaf upside-down and tap it gently on the base. If it sounds hollow, the bread is cooked.

MAKING APRICOT GLAZE

To make a glaze to brush over fresh fruit on cakes or tarts, place a few spoonfuls of apricot jam in a small pan with a squeeze of lemon juice. Heat, stirring, until the jam is melted. Pour the melted jam into a wire sieve set over a bowl and stir with a wooden spoon to help it go through. Return the strained jam glaze to the pan and keep it warm while brushing it generously over the fruit.

Savoury Buns & Scones

Oatcakes

INGREDIENTS

175g/6oz/1⅔ cups oatmeal
75g/3oz/¾ cup plain flour
1.5ml/¼ tsp bicarbonate of soda
5ml/1 tsp salt
25g/1oz/2 tbsp bacon fat or vegetable fat
25g/1oz/2 tbsp butter

MAKES 24

1 Preheat the oven to 220°C/425°F/Gas 7. Place the oatmeal, flour, bicarbonate of soda and salt in a large bowl. Gently melt the bacon or vegetable fat and butter together in a saucepan.

2 Add the melted fat to the dry ingredients, together with enough boiling water to make a soft dough. Knead together and turn out on to a surface scattered with a

little oatmeal. Roll out the dough thinly and cut it into circles with a plain biscuit cutter. Bake the oatcakes on ungreased baking sheets for 15 minutes, until crisp.

Wholemeal Herb Triangles

INGREDIENTS

225g/8oz/2 cups wholemeal flour
115g/4oz/1 cup strong plain flour
5ml/1 tsp salt
2.5ml/½ tsp bicarbonate of soda
5ml/1 tsp cream of tartar
2.5ml/½ tsp chilli powder
50g/2oz/¼ cup butter
60ml/4 tbsp chopped mixed fresh herbs
250ml/8fl oz/1 cup skimmed milk
15ml/1 tbsp sesame seeds

MAKES 8

1 Preheat the oven to 220°C/425°F/Gas 7. Lightly flour a baking sheet. Put the wholemeal flour in a mixing bowl. Sift in the remaining dry ingredients, including the chilli powder, then rub in the butter.

2 Add the herbs and milk and mix quickly to a soft dough. Turn on to a lightly floured surface. Knead only very briefly or the dough will become tough. Roll out to a 23cm/9in round and place on the prepared baking sheet. Brush lightly with water and sprinkle evenly with the sesame seeds.

3 Carefully cut the dough round into 8 wedges, separate them slightly and bake for 15–20 minutes. Transfer to a wire rack to cool. Serve warm or cold.

Drop Scones

INGREDIENTS

225g/8oz/2 cups self-raising flour
2.5ml/½ tsp salt
15ml/1 tbsp caster sugar
1 egg, beaten
300ml/½ pint/1¼ cups skimmed milk

MAKES 18

2 Add the egg and half the milk to the bowl, then gradually incorporate the surrounding flour to make a smooth batter. Beat in the remaining milk.

3 Lightly grease the griddle or heavy-based frying pan. Drop tablespoons of the batter on to the surface, leaving them until they bubble and the bubbles begin to burst.

4 Turn the drop scones over with a palette knife and cook until the underside is golden brown. Keep the cooked drop scones warm and moist by wrapping them in a clean tea-towel while cooking successive batches.

1 Preheat a griddle, heavy-based frying pan or electric frying pan. Sift the flour and salt into a mixing bowl. Stir in the sugar and make a well in the centre.

VARIATION

For savoury scones, omit the sugar and add 2 chopped spring onions and 15ml/1 tbsp freshly grated Parmesan cheese to the batter.

Parmesan Popovers

INGREDIENTS

50g / 2oz freshly grated Parmesan cheese
115g / 4oz / 1 cup plain flour
pinch of salt
2 eggs
125ml / 4fl oz / ½ cup milk
15ml / 1 tbsp melted butter

MAKES 6

2 Sift the flour and salt into a small bowl and set aside. In a mixing bowl, beat together the eggs, milk and butter. Add the flour mixture and stir until smoothly blended.

3 Divide the mixture evenly among the tins, filling each one half full. Bake for 15 minutes, then sprinkle the tops of the popovers with the remaining grated  Parmesan. Reduce the heat to 180°C/350°F/ Gas 4 and continue baking for a further 10 minutes, until the popovers are firm and golden brown.

4 Remove the popovers from the oven and turn out, running a thin knife around the inside of each tin to loosen the popovers. Serve immediately.

1 Preheat the oven to 230°C/450°F/ Gas 8. Grease six deep bun or tartlet tins, then sprinkle each tin with 30ml/2 tbsp of the grated Parmesan and set aside.

COOK'S TIP
If you don't have any deep bun tins,
you can use ramekins. Heat them on a baking
sheet in the oven, then grease and sprinkle with
Parmesan just before filling with the mixture.

16

Cheese Muffins

INGREDIENTS

*50g/2oz butter, plus extra for greasing
(optional)
200g/7oz/1¾ cups plain flour
10ml/2 tsp baking powder
30ml/2 tbsp sugar
pinch of salt
5ml/1 tsp paprika
2 eggs
125ml/4fl oz/½ cup milk
5ml/1 tsp dried thyme, roughly chopped
50g/2oz mature Cheddar cheese, cut into
1cm/½in cubes*

MAKES 9

1 Preheat the oven to 190°C/375°F/Gas 5. Thickly grease 9 deep muffin or bun tins or use paper muffin cases.

2 Melt the butter and set aside. In a large mixing bowl, sift together the plain flour, baking powder, sugar, salt and paprika.

3 In another bowl, combine the eggs, milk, melted butter and chopped thyme, and whisk to blend.

4 Add the milk mixture to the dry ingredients in the mixing bowl and stir until moistened — do not attempt to mix until smooth.

5 Place a heaped spoonful of batter in each muffin tin. Drop a few cubes of the Cheddar cheese into each tin, then top with another generous spoonful of batter.

6 Bake for 25 minutes or until the muffins are puffed and golden. Leave the muffins in the tins for 5 minutes before turning out on to a wire rack. Serve warm.

COOK'S TIP
*For even baking, half-fill any empty
muffin cups with water before
putting them in the oven.*

Ham & Tomato Scones

INGREDIENTS

225g/8oz/2 cups self-raising flour
5ml/1 tsp dry mustard
5ml/1 tsp paprika, plus extra for sprinkling
2.5ml/½ tsp salt
25g/1oz/2 tbsp butter
15ml/1 tbsp snipped fresh basil
50g/2oz/⅓ cup sun-dried tomatoes in oil,
drained and chopped
50g/2oz pre-cooked ham, chopped
90–120ml/3–4fl oz/½–⅔ cup skimmed
milk, plus extra for brushing

MAKES 12

1 Preheat the oven to 200°C/400°F/ Gas 6. Flour a large baking sheet. Sift the flour, mustard, paprika and salt into a large bowl. Rub in the butter until the mixture resembles breadcrumbs.

2 Stir in the snipped fresh basil, sun-dried tomatoes and chopped ham, and mix together lightly. Pour in enough milk to mix to a soft dough.

3 Turn out the dough on to a lightly floured surface, knead lightly and roll out to a 20 x 15cm/ 8 x 6in rectangle. Cut into 5cm/2in squares and arrange on the prepared baking sheet.

4 Brush the dough lightly with milk, sprinkle with a little paprika and bake for 12–15 minutes in the preheated oven. Transfer to a wire rack to cool.

Chive & Potato Scones

INGREDIENTS

450g / 1lb potatoes
115g / 4oz / 1 cup plain flour, sifted
30ml / 2 tbsp olive oil
30ml / 2 tbsp snipped fresh chives
salt and freshly ground black pepper

MAKES 20

1 Cook the potatoes in a large pan of boiling salted water for 20 minutes or until tender, then drain thoroughly. Return the potatoes to the pan and mash them. Preheat a griddle or heavy-based frying pan.

2 Add the flour, olive oil and snipped chives, with a little salt and pepper, to the mashed potato. Mix to a soft dough.

3 Roll out the dough on a well-floured surface to a thickness of 5mm/¹⁄4in, and stamp out rounds with a 5cm/2in plain cutter. Lightly grease the griddle or frying pan.

4 Cook the scones in batches over a low heat for about 10 minutes, turning once, until golden brown on both sides. Serve the scones immediately, with butter.

21

Preserves & Spreads

Tomato Chutney

INGREDIENTS

900g / 2lb tomatoes
225g / 8oz onions
225g / 8oz / 1⅓ cups raisins
225g / 8oz / 1⅛ cups caster sugar
600ml / 1 pint / 2½ cups malt vinegar

MAKES 1.75KG/4LB

1 Put the tomatoes in a large bowl and pour over boiling water. Leave for 30 seconds, then plunge into cold water. Peel, seed and roughly chop the tomatoes. Put them into a preserving pan.

2 Use a sharp knife to chop the onions roughly, and then add them to the preserving pan. Add the raisins and the caster sugar.

3 Pour over the malt vinegar. Bring to the boil and leave to simmer for 2 hours, uncovered. Spoon the chutney into warmed, sterilized jars and seal immediately with waxed discs and tightly fitting plastic lids. Store in a cool, dark place. The chutney will keep, unopened, for up to a year. Once opened, store in the fridge and consume within a week.

Ploughman's Pâté with Melba Toast

INGREDIENTS

50g/2oz/3 tbsp full fat soft cheese
50g/2oz/¾ cup Caerphilly cheese, grated
50g/2oz/¾ cup Double Gloucester cheese,
grated
4 silverskin pickled onions, drained and
finely chopped
15ml/1 tbsp apricot chutney
25g/1oz/2 tbsp butter, melted
30ml/2 tbsp snipped fresh chives
salt and freshly ground black pepper
4 slices soft grain bread
watercress and cherry tomatoes, to serve

SERVES 4

1 Mix together in a bowl the soft cheese, grated cheeses, pickled onions, chutney and butter. Season lightly with salt and ground black pepper.

2 Spoon the mixture on to a sheet of greaseproof paper and roll up into a cylinder, forming a smooth shape with your hands. Scrunch the ends of the paper together and twist to seal. Put into the freezer for about 30 minutes, until just firm.

3 Spread the snipped chives on a plate, then unwrap the chilled cheese pâté. Roll it in the chives until evenly coated. Wrap the pâté in clear film and chill for 10 minutes.

4 Preheat the grill. Toast the bread lightly on both sides. Cut off the crusts and slice each piece in half horizontally. Cut each half into two triangles, then grill, untoasted side up, until golden and curled at the edges.

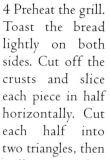

5 Slice the pâté into rounds and serve three or four rounds per person, with the Melba toast, watercress and cherry tomatoes.

Strawberry Jam

INGREDIENTS

1.5kg/3lb strawberries
1.5kg/3lb/6 cups granulated sugar
juice of ½ lemon

MAKES 2.25KG/5LB

1 Hull the strawberries and mash half of them. Warm the sugar in an ovenproof bowl in a low oven (120°C/250°F/Gas ½).

2 Put the mashed and whole strawberries in a preserving pan with the lemon juice. Simmer gently over a medium-low heat, until the fruit is just tender.

3 Add the warmed sugar and allow it to dissolve slowly over a gentle heat. Then let the jam boil rapidly until a setting point is reached. Remove from the heat.

4 Leave the jam in the preserving pan for 5 minutes, to rest, then stir until the strawberries are well distributed. Pot the jam into warmed, sterilized jars. Seal each jar immediately with a waxed disc and cover with a tightly fitting lid. Store in a cool dark place. The jam may be kept unopened for up to a year. Once opened, keep in the fridge and consume within a week.

COOK'S TIP
Test for setting by pouring about 5ml/1 tsp jam into a saucer and leaving to cool slightly. If a wrinkle forms on the surface when pushed with a fingertip, the jam will set.

Apple & Mint Jelly

INGREDIENTS

900g/2lb cooking apples
granulated sugar (see method)
45ml/3 tbsp chopped fresh mint

MAKES 1.5KG/3LB

3 Then measure the amount of juice strained from the jelly bag. For every 600ml/1 pint/ 2½ cups of juice, add 500g/1¼lb/ 2¾ cups granulated sugar.

4 Heat the juice mixture gently, stirring, to dissolve the sugar. Bring to the boil. After about 10 minutes, test for setting by pouring about 5ml/ 1 tsp into a saucer and leaving to cool slightly. If a wrinkle forms on the surface when pushed with a fingertip, the jelly will set. Leave to cool.

1 Chop the cooking apples roughly and put them into a preserving pan. Add enough cold water to cover the fruit. Simmer over a medium heat until the fruit is soft.

2 Strain the fruit through a jelly bag into a large saucepan, allowing it to drip overnight. Do not squeeze the bag or the jelly will become cloudy.

5 Stir in the chopped fresh mint and pour the jelly into warmed, sterilized jars. Seal each jar with a waxed disc and a tightly fitting plastic top. Store in a cool, dark place. The jelly will keep unopened for up to a year. Once opened, keep in the fridge and consume within a week.

Sandwiches

Rose Petal Sandwiches

INGREDIENTS

225g/8oz/1 cup unsalted butter
5 heads of scented roses, either dark pink or red
1 loaf of soft, thinly sliced white bread

SERVES 8

1 Cut the block of butter in half lengthways and place each half on a dish lined with a thick layer of rose petals. Cover the sides and top of the butter generously with more petals. Cover with a lid or layer of muslin and leave for 24 hours in the larder section of the fridge.

2 Discard the top layer of petals and allow the butter to soften slightly before spreading it on to very thin slices of bread. Use a heart-shaped pastry cutter to cut out the centre of each slice and add a thin layer of fresh rose petals before putting the slices together to make sandwiches.

COOK'S TIP
The best time of day to collect rose petals from the garden is early in the morning, when they are at their most fragrant.

33

√ Crab & Avocado Sandwiches

INGREDIENTS

175g/6oz crab meat
2 spring onions, chopped
salt and pepper
100ml/4fl oz/½ cup mayonnaise
1 large avocado, peeled and halved
15ml/1 tbsp lemon juice
50g/2oz/4 tbsp softened butter
8 slices granary bread
curly endive leaves, to garnish

MAKES 4

34

1 Mix the crab meat with the chopped spring onions in a mixing bowl. Add seasoning to taste and mix together with 30ml/2 tbsp of the mayonnaise.

2 Cut the avocado into slices and brush all over with lemon juice to prevent it from discolouring.

3 Butter the granary bread and divide the crab meat between four of the slices, spreading the mixture right to the edges. Cover the crab mixture with the slices of avocado.

4 Then spread the remaining mayonnaise over the top of the avocado slices. Cover with the remaining slices of bread and press together firmly. Cut off the crusts and cut the sandwiches diagonally into quarters. Place the sandwiches on a plate and garnish with curly endive leaves.

Sandwich Horns

INGREDIENTS

8 thin slices of brown bread
100g/4oz/½ cup cottage cheese
15ml/1 tbsp mixed chopped fresh parsley,
chives and thyme
salt and pepper
100g/4oz/½ cup each Avocado Filling and
Smoked Salmon Filling
fresh herbs, to garnish

MAKES 8

1 Remove the crusts from the brown bread and cut one corner off each slice, rounding it slightly.

2 Mix the cottage cheese and chopped herbs together in a bowl with some seasoning. Spread a slice of the bread with some of this mixture.

3 With the round-ed corner towards you, lift the two sides and fold one over the other. Stick the bread in position with the filling and secure with a cocktail  stick. Chill for 20 minutes to firm up. Repeat using the Avocado and Smoked Salmon Fillings.

4 Holding each horn upright, top up with a little more filling, using a teaspoon. Remove the cocktail sticks before serving and garnish with sprigs of fresh herbs.

AVOCADO FILLING
Peel and stone a large avocado and mash with a fork. Beat in 15ml/1 tbsp lemon juice and 15ml/1 tbsp mayonnaise. Season to taste with salt and pepper.

SMOKED SALMON FILLING
Put 50g/2oz smoked salmon pieces in a blender with 75ml/3fl oz/⅓ cup double cream, 5ml/1 tsp lemon juice and a little ground black pepper. Blend briefly to a rough purée.

Smoked Salmon Pinwheels

INGREDIENTS

1 small unsliced brown loaf
1 small lemon
75g/3oz/6 tbsp softened butter
15ml/1 tbsp chopped fresh dill
225g/8oz smoked salmon slices
freshly ground black pepper
sprig of fresh dill, to garnish

MAKES 56

1 Slice the brown loaf carefully along its length to form 8 thin slices. Cut off the crusts.

2 Grate the lemon zest finely and beat into the butter with the dill.

3 Spread each slice of bread with the lemon-flavoured butter and arrange smoked salmon slices over the bread, leaving a strip of buttered bread at one short end. Grind some black pepper over the top.

4 With the salmon-covered short end towards you, roll up the bread carefully and tightly like a Swiss roll. The buttered end will ensure that the bread sticks together.

5 Wrap each roll in clear film and chill for 1 hour. This will help the filling and bread to set in the rolled position so that it does not unwind when sliced.

6 Using a sharp bread knife, carefully cut each roll into 1cm/½in slices. Arrange the slices attractively on a plate and serve garnished with a sprig of dill.

Ham & Asparagus Slice

INGREDIENTS

12 asparagus spears
100g/4oz/½ cup cream cheese
4 slices rye bread
4 slices ham
few leaves curly endive
30ml/2 tbsp mayonnaise
4 radish roses, to garnish

MAKES 4

38

1 Cook the asparagus spears in salted boiling water in a saucepan until tender. Drain the asparagus and pat dry with kitchen paper, then set aside to cool.

2 Spread cream cheese over the rye bread and arrange the ham in folds over the top of the cream cheese. Lay 3 asparagus spears on the ham on each sandwich.

3 Arrange a curly endive leaf on top and add a spoonful of mayonnaise to each sandwich. Garnish with radish roses and serve with the remaining mayonnaise.

Roquefort & Pear Brioche Slices

INGREDIENTS

4 slices brioche
125g/4oz/½ cup curd cheese
125g/4oz Roquefort cheese, sliced
few sprigs rocket
1 ripe pear, quartered, cored and sliced
juice of ½ lemon
4 pecan nuts, to garnish
viola flowers, to garnish (optional)

MAKES 4

1 Toast the brioche slices under the grill and spread them thickly with the curd cheese. Place the sliced Roquefort on top. Arrange rocket leaves on top of the cheese.

2 Brush the pear slices with lemon juice to prevent them from discolouring, then arrange them on top of the cheese, overlapping them in a fan shape.

3 Garnish the brioches slices with whole or chopped pecan nuts and a viola flower, if you wish.

39

Scrambled Egg & Salmon Muffins

INGREDIENTS

4 eggs
45ml / 3 tbsp single cream or top of the milk
4 wholemeal muffins
25g / 1oz / 2 tbsp butter, plus
extra for spreading
15ml / 1 tbsp snipped fresh chives, plus extra,
to garnish
2.5ml / ½ tsp grated lemon rind
115g / 4oz smoked salmon or trout, snipped
into strips
salt and pepper

SERVES 4

40

2 Halve the muffins and grill them until lightly toasted on both sides. Spread with a little butter and keep them warm.

3 Meanwhile, melt the butter in a saucepan over a gentle heat, add the eggs and stir occasionally with a wooden spoon until the eggs are just beginning to set.

4 Add the chives to the eggs in the saucepan, and add the lemon rind and strips of smoked salmon or trout. Stir until the eggs are just set but still moist.
Spoon on to the toasted muffins and garnish with snipped fresh chives. Serve at once.

1 Break the eggs into a large mixing bowl, then pour on the cream or milk and season well with salt and pepper. Beat the mixture lightly with a fork.

COOK'S TIP

It is important not to overcook the scrambled eggs — remove the pan from the heat while the eggs are still quite creamy.

Teabreads &
Cakes

Easter Plait

INGREDIENTS

200ml/7fl oz/⅞ cup milk
2 eggs, lightly beaten
75g/3oz/6 tbsp caster sugar
450g/1lb/4 cups plain flour
2.5ml/½ tsp salt
10ml/2 tsp ground mixed spice
75g/3oz/6 tbsp butter
20g/¾ oz fresh yeast
175g/6oz/1¼ cups currants
25g/1oz/¼ cup candied mixed peel, chopped
a little sweetened milk, to glaze
25g/1oz/1½ tbsp glacé cherries, chopped
15g/½oz/1 tbsp angelica, chopped

SERVES 8

1 Heat the milk in a saucepan until it is lukewarm, then add two-thirds of it to the eggs and mix in the caster sugar.

2 Sift the flour, salt and mixed spice together in a large bowl. Rub in the butter. Make a well in the centre. Add the milk mixture and yeast, adding more milk as necessary to make a sticky dough.

3 Knead on a well-floured surface and then knead in the currants and mixed peel, reserving 15ml/ 1 tbsp peel for the topping. Put the dough in a lightly greased bowl and cover it with a damp cloth. Leave until doubled in size. Preheat the oven to 220°C/425°F/Gas 7.

4 Turn the dough out on to a floured surface and knead again for 2–3 minutes. Divide the dough into three equal pieces. Roll each piece into a sausage shape roughly 20cm/8in long. Plait the three pieces together, turning under and pinching each end. Place on a floured baking sheet and leave to rise for 15 minutes.

5 Brush the top of the plait with a little sweetened milk and scatter with roughly chopped glacé cherries, small strips of angelica and the reserved mixed peel. Bake the plait in the preheated oven for about 45 minutes or until the loaf sounds hollow when tapped on the bottom. Leave to cool on a wire rack.

43

Banana & Ginger Teabread

INGREDIENTS

175g/6oz/1½ cups self-raising flour
5ml/1 tsp baking powder
40g/1½oz/3 tbsp butter
50g/2oz/⅓ cup dark muscovado sugar
50g/2oz/⅓ cup drained stem ginger, chopped
60ml/4 tbsp milk
2 ripe bananas

SERVES 6–8

44

1 Preheat the oven to 180°C/350°F/Gas 4. Grease and line a 450g/1lb loaf tin. Sift the flour and baking powder into a large mixing bowl.

2 Rub the butter into the dry ingredients in the mixing bowl until the mixture resembles breadcrumbs.

3 Stir in the sugar. Add the milk and chopped ginger. Mash the bananas and add to the contents of the bowl. Mix together until a soft dough is formed.

4 Spoon into the prepared tin and bake for 40–45 minutes. Run a palette knife around the edges to loosen them, turn the teabread on to a wire rack and leave to cool. Serve sliced, spread with butter.

Irish Whiskey Cake

INGREDIENTS

115g/4oz/⅔ cup glacé cherries, roughly chopped
175g/6oz/1 cup dark muscovado sugar
115g/4oz/⅔ cup sultanas
115g/4oz/⅔ cup raisins
115g/4oz/½ cup currants
300ml/½ pint/1¼ cups cold tea
300g/10oz/2½ cups self-raising flour, sifted
1 egg
45ml/3 tbsp Irish whiskey

SERVES 12

1 Mix the cherries, sugar, dried fruit and tea in a large bowl. Leave to soak overnight until all the tea has been absorbed into the fruit.

2 Preheat the oven to 180°C/350°F/ Gas 4. Grease and line a 1kg/2¼lb loaf tin. Add the flour, then the egg to the fruit mixture and beat thoroughly until well mixed.

3 Pour the mixture into the prepared tin and bake for 1½ hours or until a skewer inserted into the centre of the cake comes out clean.

4 Prick the top of the cake with a skewer and drizzle over the whiskey while the cake is still hot. Allow the cake to stand for about 5 minutes, then turn out of the loaf tin. Allow the cake to cool on a wire rack before serving.

Pound Cake with Red Fruit

INGREDIENTS

450g/1lb fresh raspberries, strawberries or
stoned cherries, or a combination of any of these
175g/6oz/⅞ cup caster sugar, plus
15–30ml/1–2 tbsp and some for sprinkling
15ml/1 tbsp lemon juice
175g/6oz/1⅓ cups plain flour
10ml/2 tsp baking powder
pinch of salt
175g/6oz/¾ cup unsalted butter, softened
3 eggs
grated rind of 1 orange
15ml/1 tbsp orange juice

SERVES 6–8

1 Reserve a few whole fruits for decoration. Put the rest into a food processor and blend until smooth.

2 Add 15–30ml/1–2 tbsp caster sugar and the lemon juice to the fruit purée and blend again. Strain the sauce and chill in the fridge.

3 Butter the base and sides of a 20 x 10cm/8 x 4in loaf tin or a 20cm/8in springform tin and line the base with non-stick baking paper. Butter the paper and sprinkle the base and sides of the tin lightly with sugar, tipping out any excess. Preheat the oven to 180°C/350°F/Gas 4.

4 Sift the flour with the baking powder and salt. In a medium bowl, cream the butter and sugar together thoroughly until light and fluffy, then add the eggs, one at a time, beating well after each addition. Beat in the orange rind and juice.

5 Gently fold the flour mixture into the butter mixture in three batches, then spoon the mixture into the prepared tin and gently tap the sides of the tin to release any air bubbles.

6 Bake the cake for 35–40 minutes until the top is golden and springs back when touched. Transfer the cake in its tin to a wire rack and leave to cool for 10 minutes. Remove the cake from the tin and cool for about ½ hour. Remove the paper and slice the cake. Serve warm with a little of the fruit sauce, decorated with the reserved fruit.

Lavender Cake

INGREDIENTS

175g/6oz/¾ cup unsalted butter, softened
175g/6oz/⅞ cup caster sugar
3 eggs
175g/6oz/1½ cups self-raising flour, sifted
30ml/2 tbsp fresh lavender florets or 15ml/
1 tbsp dried culinary lavender, roughly chopped
2.5ml/½ tsp vanilla essence
30ml/2 tbsp milk
50g/2oz/½ cup icing sugar, sifted
2.5ml/½ tsp water
a few fresh lavender flowers

SERVES 6–8

I Preheat the oven to 180°C/350°F/Gas 4. Lightly grease and flour a ring tin or a deep 20cm/8in round, loose-based cake tin. Cream the butter and sugar together in a mixing bowl until light and fluffy, then add the eggs, one at a time, beating well after each addition. Fold in the flour, chopped lavender, vanilla essence and milk.

2 Spoon the mixture into the prepared tin and bake in the oven for 1 hour. Leave to stand for 5 minutes, then turn out on to a wire rack to cool.

3 Mix the icing sugar with the water until smooth. Pour the icing over the cake and decorate with a few fresh lavender flowers.

Cinnamon Apple Gâteau

INGREDIENTS

3 eggs
115g/4oz/½ cup caster sugar
75g/3oz/¾ cup plain flour
5ml/1 tsp ground cinnamon

FILLING AND TOPPING
4 large eating apples
60ml/4 tbsp clear honey
15ml/1 tbsp water
75g/3oz/½ cup sultanas
2.5ml/½ tsp ground cinnamon
350g/12oz/1½ cups low fat soft cheese
60ml/4 tbsp fromage frais
10ml/2 tsp lemon juice
45ml/3 tbsp Apricot Glaze
mint sprigs, to decorate

SERVES 8

1 Preheat the oven to 190°C/375°F/Gas 5. Grease and line a 23cm/9in round cake tin. Place the eggs and caster sugar in a bowl and beat until thick and mousse-like (when the whisk is lifted, a trail should remain on the surface of the mixture for at least 15 seconds).

2 Sift the flour and cinnamon over the egg mixture and carefully fold in with a large spoon. Pour into the prepared tin and bake for 25–30 minutes or until the cake springs back when lightly pressed. Slide a palette knife between the cake and the tin to loosen the edge, then turn the cake on to a wire rack to cool.

3 To make the filling, peel, core and slice three of the apples and put them in a saucepan. Add 30ml/2 tbsp of the honey and the water. Cover and cook over a gentle heat for about 10 minutes until the apples have softened. Add the sultanas and cinnamon, stir well, replace the lid and leave to cool.

4 Put the soft cheese in a bowl with the remaining honey, the fromage frais, and half the lemon juice. Beat together until the mixture is smooth.

5 Halve the cake horizontally, place the bottom half on a board and drizzle over any liquid from the apples. Spread with two-thirds of the cheese mixture, then top with the apple filling. Fit the top of the cake in place.

6 Swirl the remaining cheese mixture over the top of the sponge. Core and slice the remaining apple, sprinkle it with lemon juice, to prevent it from discolouring, and use it to decorate the edge of the cake. Brush the apple with Apricot Glaze and place mint sprigs on top, to decorate.

Rich Chocolate Cake

INGREDIENTS

250g/9oz plain chocolate, chopped
225g/8oz/1 cup unsalted butter, diced
5 eggs
100g/3½oz/½ cup caster sugar, plus
15ml/1 tbsp and some for sprinkling
15ml/1 tbsp cocoa powder, plus extra,
for dusting
10ml/2 tsp vanilla essence
chocolate shavings, to decorate

SERVES 14–16

50

1 Preheat the oven to 160°C/325°F/Gas 3. Lightly butter a 23cm/9in springform tin and line the base with non-stick baking paper. Butter the paper and sprinkle with a little sugar, then tip out the excess.

2 The cake is baked in a bain-marie, so carefully wrap the base and sides of the tin in a double thickness of foil to prevent water leaking into the cake.

3 Melt the chocolate with the butter in a saucepan over a low heat until smooth, stirring frequently, then remove from the heat. Beat the eggs with 100g/3½oz/½ cup sugar until light and thick.

4 Mix together the cocoa and the remaining 15ml/1 tbsp sugar and beat into the egg mixture until well blended. Beat in the vanilla essence, then slowly beat in the melted chocolate until well blended. Pour the mixture into the prepared tin and tap gently to release any air bubbles.

5 Place the cake tin in a roasting tin and pour in boiling water to come 2cm/¾in up the sides of the wrapped tin. Bake for 45–50 minutes until the edge  of the cake is set and the centre is still soft (a skewer inserted 5cm/2in from the edge should come out clean). Lift the tin out of the water and remove the foil. Place the cake on a wire rack, remove the sides of the tin and leave to cool completely (the cake will sink a little in the centre).

6 Invert the cake on to the wire rack. Remove the base of the tin and the paper. Dust with cocoa powder and decorate with chocolate shavings.

Biscuits, Tarts & Sweet Scones

Greek Festival Shortbreads

INGREDIENTS

250g/9oz/1 generous cup unsalted butter
65g/2½oz/⅓ cup caster sugar
1 egg yolk
30ml/2 tbsp Greek ouzo, Pernod or brandy
115g/4oz/1½ cups unblanched almonds
65g/2½oz/generous ½ cup cornflour
300g/11oz/2¼ cups plain flour
60ml/4 tbsp triple-distilled rose-water
500g/1¼lb/2¾ cups icing sugar, sifted

MAKES 24–28

1 Preheat the oven to 180°C/350°F/Gas 4. In a mixing bowl, cream the butter and add the caster sugar, egg yolk and alcohol.

2 Grind the almonds in their skins: they should be much coarser and browner than commercially ground almonds. Add to the butter mixture, then stir in the cornflour and enough plain flour to give a firm, soft dough. (You may need to add a little more flour.)

3 Line two large baking sheets with non-stick baking paper. Divide the dough into 24–28 equal portions. Make them into little rolls, then bend them into crescents round a finger. Place on the baking sheets and bake for 15 minutes. Check the biscuits and lower the oven temperature to 170°C/325°F/Gas 3 if they seem to be colouring. Bake for a further 5–10 minutes. Remove from the oven and leave to cool.

4 Pour the rose-water into a small bowl and tip the sifted icing sugar into a larger one. Dip a biscuit into the rose-water, sprinkle it with icing sugar and place in an airtight tin. Repeat until all the biscuits are coated. Pack the biscuits loosely to prevent them sticking together. Sift the remaining icing sugar over the biscuits and keep them in the airtight tin until needed.

53

√ Spiced Nut Palmiers

INGREDIENTS

75g/3oz/½ cup chopped almonds, walnuts or
hazelnuts
30ml/2 tbsp caster sugar, plus extra
for sprinkling
2.5ml/½ tsp ground cinnamon
225g/½lb puff pastry
1 egg, lightly beaten

MAKES ABOUT 40

1 Lightly butter two large baking sheets, preferably non-stick. In a food processor, process the nuts, sugar and cinnamon until finely ground. Transfer half the mixture to a small bowl.

2 Sprinkle the work surface and pastry with caster sugar and roll out the pastry to a 50 x 20cm/20 x 8in rectangle about 3mm/⅛in thick, sprinkling with  more sugar as necessary. Brush the pastry lightly with beaten egg, and sprinkle evenly with the nut mixture in the bowl.

3 Fold in the long edges of the pastry to meet in the centre and flatten with the rolling pin. Brush with egg and sprinkle with most of the remaining nut mixture. Fold in the edges again to meet in the centre, brush with egg and sprinkle with the remaining nut mixture. Fold one side of the pastry over the other.

4 Using a sharp knife, cut the pastry crossways into 8mm/⅜in thick slices and place the pieces cut-side down about 2.5cm/1in apart on the prepared baking sheets.

5 Spread apart the pastry edges to form a wedge shape. Chill the palmiers in the fridge for at least 15–20 minutes. Preheat the oven to 220°C/425°F/ Gas 7.

6 Bake the palmiers in the preheated oven for about 8–10 minutes until golden, carefully turning them over halfway through the cooking time. Watch the palmiers carefully as the sugar can easily scorch. Transfer them to a wire rack to cool. Store in an airtight tin until needed.

Madeleines

INGREDIENTS

165g/5½oz/1¼ cups plain flour
5·rl 1 tsp baking powder
2 eggs
75g/3oz/¾ cup icing sugar, plus extra
for dusting
grated rind of 1 lemon or orange
15ml/1 tbsp lemon or orange juice
75g/3oz/6 tbsp unsalted butter, melted and
slightly cooled

MAKES 12

3 Fold in the citrus rind and juice. Beginning with the flour mixture, alternately fold in the flour and butter in four batches. Let the mixture stand for

10 minutes, then spoon it into the tin. Tap to release any air bubbles. Bake the madeleines for about 12–15 minutes, rotating the tin halfway through cooking, until a skewer inserted in the centre comes out clean. Turn out on to a wire rack to cool and dust with icing sugar.

1 Preheat the oven to 190°C/375°F/Gas 5. Generously butter a 12-cup madeleine tin. Sift together the flour and baking powder in a bowl.

2 Beat the eggs and icing sugar together until the mixture is thick and creamy and forms a ribbon when the whisk is lifted.

56

Strawberry Tart

INGREDIENTS

350g/¾lb puff pastry
225g/½lb cream cheese
grated rind of ½ orange
30ml/2 tbsp orange liqueur or orange juice
45–60ml/3–4 tbsp icing sugar, plus extra
for dusting (optional)
450g/1lb ripe strawberries, hulled

SERVES 6

1 Roll out the pastry to a thickness of about 3mm/⅛in and use to line a 28 x 10cm/11 x 4in rectangular flan tin. Trim the edges, then chill for 20–30 minutes. Preheat the oven to 200°C/400°F/Gas 6.

2 Prick the base of the pastry all over with a fork. Line the pastry case with foil, fill with baking beans and bake for 15 minutes. Remove the beans and foil and bake for a further 10 minutes until the pastry is browned. Gently press down on the pastry base to deflate, then leave to cool on a wire rack.

3 Beat together the cream cheese, orange rind, liqueur or orange juice and add icing sugar to taste. Spread the cheese filling in the pastry case. Halve the strawberries and arrange them on top of the cheese filling. Dust the tart with icing sugar, if you wish.

Fruits of the Forest Pavlova

INGREDIENTS

4 egg whites
175g/6oz/¾ cup caster sugar
60ml/4 tbsp rose or redcurrant jelly
300ml/½ pint/1¼ cups thick double cream
or fromage frais
300g/11oz/2¾ cups mixed soft fruits
fresh and crystallized rose petals for decoration

SERVES 4–6

58

1 Preheat the oven to 140°C/275°F/ Gas 1. Then draw a 20cm/8in circle on non-stick baking paper. Turn over the paper so the marking is on the other side and use it to line a heavy baking sheet.

2 Whisk the egg whites in a grease-free bowl until very stiff and slowly whisk in the caster sugar until the mixture makes stiff, glossy peaks. Spoon the meringue on to the baking paper on the baking sheet, making a slight indentation in the centre and soft crests around the outside.

3 Bake in the oven for 1–1½ hours until the meringue is crisp, taking care not to let it brown. Leave the meringue to cool in the oven.

4 Immediately before serving, melt the jelly over a low heat and spread in the centre of the meringue nest. Spoon over the cream or fromage frais and arrange the soft fruits and rose petals on top. The dish should be eaten straight away.

COOK'S TIP
When making the meringue, whisk the egg whites until they are so stiff that you can turn the bowl upside down without them falling out.

Raspberry Muffins

INGREDIENTS

275g/10oz/2½ cups plain flour
15ml/1 tbsp baking powder
115g/4oz/½ cup caster sugar
1 egg
250ml/8fl oz/1 cup buttermilk
60ml/4 tbsp sunflower oil
150g/5oz/1 cup raspberries

MAKES 10–12

1 Preheat the oven to 200°C/400°F/Gas 6. Arrange 12 paper cases in a deep muffin tin. Sift the flour and baking powder into a large bowl, stir in the sugar, then make a well in the centre.

2 Mix the egg, buttermilk and sunflower oil together in a small bowl, then pour into the flour mixture and mix quickly until just combined.

3 Add the raspberries and lightly fold in, using a metal dessert spoon. Spoon the mixture into the paper cases to within a third of the top.

4 Bake the muffins for 20–25 minutes until golden brown and firm in the middle. Transfer to a wire rack to cool. Serve warm or cold.

Date and Apple Muffins

INGREDIENTS

150g/5oz/1¼ cups self-raising wholemeal
flour
150g/5oz/1¼ cups self-raising white flour
5ml/1 tsp ground cinnamon
5ml/1 tsp baking powder
25g/1oz/2 tbsp butter
75g/3oz/½ cup light muscovado sugar
1 eating apple
250ml/8fl oz/1 cup apple juice
30ml/2 tbsp pear and apple spread
1 egg, lightly beaten
75g/3oz/½ cup chopped dates
15ml/1 tbsp chopped pecan nuts

MAKES 12

1 Preheat the oven to 200°C/400°F/Gas 6. Arrange 12 paper cases in a deep muffin tin. Put the wholemeal flour in a mixing bowl. Sift in the white flour with the cinnamon and baking powder. Rub in the butter until the mixture resembles breadcrumbs, then stir in the muscovado sugar.

2 Quarter and core the apple, chop the flesh finely and set aside. Stir a little of the apple juice into the pear and apple spread until smooth. Mix in the remaining juice, then add to the rubbed-in mixture with the egg. Add the chopped apple to the bowl with the dates. Mix quickly until just combined.

3 Divide the mixture equally among the paper cases in the muffin tin. Sprinkle with the chopped pecan nuts. Bake the muffins in the preheated oven for 20–25 minutes until golden brown and firm in the middle. Remove to a wire rack to cool slightly and serve while still warm.

61

Orange & Raisin Scones

INGREDIENTS

285g/10oz/2½ cups plain flour
25ml/1½ tbsp baking powder
65g/2½ oz/⅓ cup caster sugar
2.5ml/½ tsp salt
150g/5oz/⅔ cup butter, diced
grated rind of 1 large orange
50g/2oz/¼ cup raisins
125ml/4fl oz/½ cup buttermilk
milk, for glazing

MAKES 16

1 Preheat the oven to 220°C/425°F/Gas 7. Grease and flour a large baking sheet.

2 Combine the dry ingredients in a large mixing bowl. Add the butter and rub in until the mixture resembles fine breadcrumbs.

3 Add the orange rind and raisins, and gradually stir in the buttermilk to form a soft dough.

4 Roll out the dough on a floured surface to a thickness of about 2cm/¾in. Stamp out circles of dough with a plain pastry cutter.

5 Place the dough circles on the prepared baking sheet and brush the tops with milk.

6 Bake for 12–15 minutes until golden. Serve hot or warm, with butter or whipped or clotted cream, and jam or honey.

Lavender Scones

INGREDIENTS

225g/8oz/2 cups plain flour
15ml/1 tbsp baking powder
50g/2oz/4 tbsp butter
50g/2oz/¼ cup sugar
10ml/2 tsp fresh lavender florets or 5ml/1tsp
dried culinary lavender, roughly chopped
150ml/¼ pint/⅔ cup milk, plus extra for
glazing

MAKES 12

1 Preheat the oven to 220°C/425°F/Gas 7. Grease and flour a large baking sheet.

2 Sift the flour and baking powder together into a large mixing bowl. Rub in the butter until the mixture resembles fine breadcrumbs. Stir in the sugar and lavender, reserving a pinch to sprinkle on the top of the scones before baking them. Add enough milk to make a soft, sticky dough, then turn it out on to a well-floured surface.

3 Shape the dough into a round about 2.5cm/1in thick. Using a round pastry cutter, stamp out 12 scones. Place the scones on the prepared baking sheet. Brush the tops with a little milk and sprinkle over the reserved chopped lavender. Bake in the preheated oven for 10–12 minutes until golden. Serve warm with whipped cream and jam.

Index